Saint Patrick Was a Cajun

61 New Irish Traditional Compositions by L.E. McCullough
All Musick Contained Herein suited to Divers Instruments

Chordal arrangements furnished by T.H. Gillespie *Esquire*

Editio Ossianum, Corcagiensis, Hiberniæ
MCMXCVIII

OSSIAN

Music typesetting by L.E.McCullough
Cover Design and Layout by John Loesberg
Special thanks to T.H.Gillespie and Dave McCumiskey

Printed by Colour Books, Dublin

Ossian Publications publish and distribute a huge range of
Irish, Scottish and other music in Print, Sound and Vision.
For our complete catalogue please send us your name and
address with an (international) postal reply coupon.

● A Double CD (Ossian OSSCD 110/111)
   with all the tunes in this book is also available.

Ossian Publications, P.O. Box 84,
Cork, Ireland.
ossian@iol.ie

OMB 139
ISBN 1 900428 46 6

This book could not exist without the genius
of traditional musicians who have gone before;
I learned everything I know from ceoltóirí kind enough
to pass on their art, and I hope this book may
in some small way repay their efforts.

Dedicated to my parents and my wife, Jane

L.E. McCullough

Contents

Composition in Traditional Irish Music
by *L.E. McCullough*

"It is the power of music to carry one directly into the mental state of the composer.
The listener has no choice. It is like hypnotism."
Ludwig Van Beethoven

"Irish music. . . it's the only music that brings people to their senses, I think."
Joe Cooley

There are at least ten thousand, maybe as many as fifteen to twenty thousand dance tunes and airs in the current canon of traditional Irish music, most of them created during the 17th, 18th and early 19th centuries and then continually shaped and re-shaped as they passed from one musician to another, from one county to another, from one continent to another. Except in a very few instances — perhaps four hundred at most — the actual composers of these tunes are completely forgotten; in some cases even these attributions may have been erroneous, with folklore taking precedence over historical fact.

It is a fact, however, that *all* the tunes played by contemporary Irish musicians were composed by *somebody*. Original composition in traditional Irish music never completely stopped, and today new tunes are still being composed, disseminated even more rapidly via recordings, movies and videos, desktop publishing, the Internet and the ability of musicians to perform globally before audiences reaching into the millions. At the end of the 20th century, it is possible to document composers of traditional Irish music and their composition processes with a much greater degree of certainty than ever before.

Composition in a traditional idiom such as Irish music presents a paradox. To be accepted as traditional, a new tune must retain enough links with the root idiom to essentially pass unnoticed as part of the already established tradition; yet it must also have something novel that makes it immediately distinctive, or else it won't pique the interest of traditional players and won't be learned or passed on. It has to be perceptibly new, but not too radically removed from the other tunes of its type. During the last twenty years or so, new compositions identified as such have appeared with increasing frequency on recordings by traditional Irish musicians. Many of these new tunes have been learned by other players, circulated via live performance and other recordings, and thus established in the active repertoire.

Are these new tunes fully "traditional"? If accepted by other traditional players and played as part of regular traditional performance occasions such as sessions, concerts and dances, a new tune soon acquires a *de facto* legitimacy. Tunes such as *Christmas Eve* by Tommy Coen, *The Golden Keyboard* by Martin Mulhare and *The Hunter's House* by Ed Reavy were composed within the last few decades and have entered the mainstream tunestock of Irish musicians worldwide; most musicians who play these tunes don't know who composed them and may not even realize they are any more recent than tunes from the 17th, 18th or 19th centuries.

Composition in Irish music has long been shrouded in mystery and folklore. Early Irish mythological tales describe three types of music characterized by function: *goltraí* (inducing sorrow in the listener), *geantraí* (inducing laughter), *suantraí* (inducing sleep). Music is presumed to have simply occurred in the mind of the musician simultaneous to being transmitted through an instrument. From the 11th to 16th centuries, though several first-hand accounts survive of performances by bardic harpers, there is again no precise description of how these musicians created their tunes.

Twenty-three tunes ascribed to the harper Turlough Carolan (1670-1738) appeared in *A Collection of the Most Celebrated Irish Tunes* published in 1726 by John and William Neale of Dublin, the first printed attribution of Irish tunes to an identifiable composer. In 1780 another Dublin publisher, John Lee, brought out a Carolan tune collection comprising sixty-eight tunes titled *A Favorite Collection of the So Much Admired Irish Tunes, the Original and Genuine Compositions of Carolan, the Celebrated Irish Bard*. Also in the mid-18th century a County Limerick uilleann piper named Walter "Piper" Jackson was noted as a composer of jigs and reels, among them *Jackson's Delight* now commonly called *The Irish Washwoman*; a collection of his compositions, *Jackson's Celebrated Irish Tunes*, was published in 1774 by Edmund Lee of Dublin. And between 1800 and 1810 a London piper named O'Farrell published at least five Irish tunebooks and uilleann pipe tutors with several of the tunes (the slip jig *O'Farrell's Welcome to Limerick* for one) likely composed by the author himself.

Collections of Irish music continued to be published throughout the 19th and early 20th centuries, many containing tunes written down directly from performers (who may in some instances have been the composers as well). Though some tunes possessed elaborate anecdotes or legends concerning their composition and transmission, there was little interest among scholars in the composers themselves or the actual composition process until 1958 when Donal O'Sullivan's two-volume book *Carolan: The Life, Times and Music of an Irish Harper* appeared. By the mid-1960s Carolan's tunes were being widely recorded and performed by ensembles such as Ceoltóirí Chualann and The Chieftains, and the long-dead harper had become one of the most well-known names in the contemporary Irish music milieu. At this point in time, it is safe to assert that every player of Irish music knows at least one Carolan tune.

In 1971 fiddler Ed Reavy of Philadelphia published *Where the Shannon Rises*, a book containing seventy-eight of his original dance tunes composed between 1927-1969. Reavy had made commercial recordings in the 1920s, and his tunes circulated among Irish musicians through-out the U.S. and in Ireland and England. Several were adopted into the tradition and recorded by musicians in the 1960s and '70s; an album of his tunes played by himself and others was released on Rounder Records in 1982 (*Ed Reavy*, Rounder Records 6008), and numerous articles on Reavy and his compositional style have been written.

In 1980 Chicago concertina/accordion player Terry Teahan, who as a boy had been a musical pupil of the famed Kerry fiddler Patrick O'Keefe, published *The Road to Glountane*, a book containing sixty-three tunes by himself and six other American Irish musicians. Cork piper Tomás Ó Canainn published a collection of fifty original Irish dance tunes in 1985 titled *New Tunes for Old*. In 1987 *The New Tradition, Volume I*, with thirty-seven new Irish tunes by sixteen American Irish composers, was published by mandolinist John Liestman of Houston. In 1993 Leitrim fiddler/pianist Charlie Lennon published a book and record album of thirty of his original tunes, *Musical Memories*.

The appearance of these collections during the 1980s and early '90s, along with occasional publication of new tunes in *Treoir* magazine, the official organ of Comhaltas Ceoltóirí Éireann, were paralleled by scores of new tunes issued on hundreds of recordings by Irish traditional musicians. With the recent emergence of the Internet, new tunes pop up weekly on web pages and in user groups and receive extended dissemination throughout the world, sometimes within hours of their composing.

Why the sudden proliferation of new tunes in this ancient idiom? Aren't there enough tunes already, more than any single musician could possibly learn in two lifetimes? Ed Reavy once said that he composed new tunes because the repertoire among musicians in his locality was becoming "a bit stale". And for traditional musicians competing in the commercial entertainment milieu, composing their own material emphasizes individuality and expands notoriety.

Then again, maybe it's just the fundamental desire humans have to leave something of themselves behind. You do it because you *can*. Because it's fun. Because it's a challenge to do right. Because it's part of the tradition, and by composing a new tune, you offer tribute to those stalwart musicians who came before you. Making a new tune is your chance to give something back, even if nobody but you ever hears it or plays it.

New composition is how the tradition stays fresh and alive. And who knows — a century or two from now when scholars discuss the "golden age of Irish traditional music", they may include our times as well as those of Carolan and Piper Jackson.

A Few Words about Music Notation

What you have here are the bare bones of the tune melody plus some suggested chords. Most players who use this book will know how to "translate" the melodic line into "real" Irish music, i.e. music played in the standard traditional style. If you don't know, find some players who do and learn from them. The only ornamention used is to indicate long and short rolls. If you want to hear how these tunes sound "live", listen to the recording that accompanies this book and always feel free to insert your own ornamentation and variations.

Keyboardist T.H. Gillespie put in some possible chords; the harmonic structure of Irish music is quite variable and there is a lot of latitude, so again use your imagination or consult books like *Traditional Irish Guitar, The Irish DADGAD Guitar Book* or *Chords for Mandolin, Irish Banjo and Bouzouki* — all by Ossian Publications.

Aside from standard major and minor chords, this book uses the following symbols:

symbol	notes
D/F#	D major with F# in the bass
Dsus2+4	DEGA
Emsus2+4	EF#AB
Dsus4	DEG
Dsus2/A	DEA with A in the bass
Emsus4/D	EAB with D in the bass

With a suspended chord like **Dsus2+4**, you're taking out the third note of the scale (F#) and putting in the second (E) and fourth (G) scale notes. When a chord is in parentheses — (**Bm**) for instance — it means it could be played at that point in the tune or not, depending upon your discretion.

The Sporting Lass of Perth (Reel)

A Snake is a Chiropractor's Dream (Reel)

Hisssssss. Photo: L.E. McCullough

How Much do Those Weigh? (Reel)

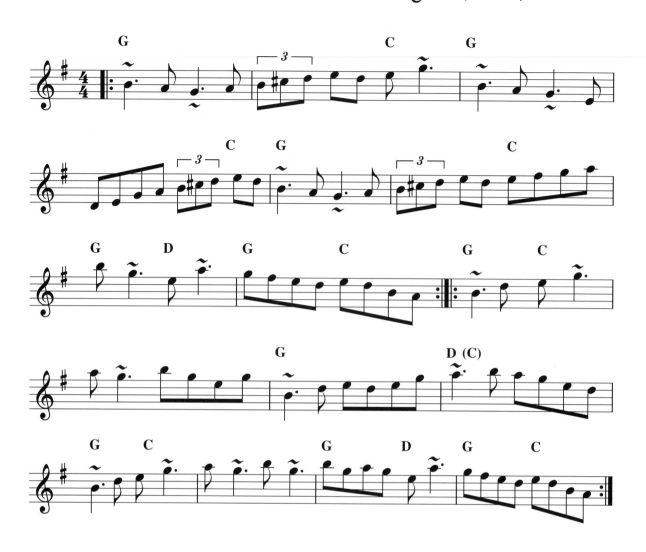

Leroy the Barbarian (Reel)

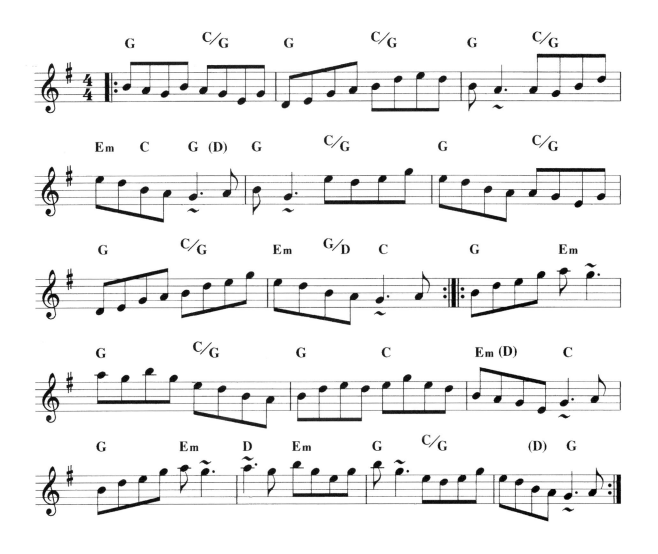

Corbin's Wedding (Reel)

Sorry to Meet, Happy to Part (Reel)

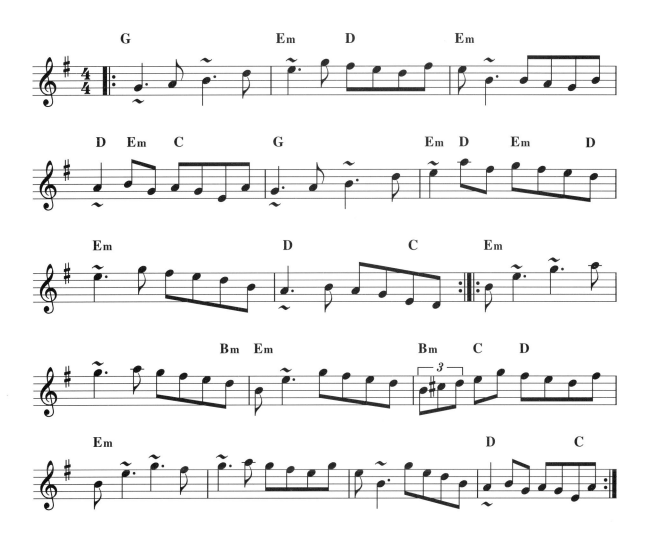

Before the D.C. Fitzgerald Farewell Reunion Concert, Jan. 26, 1981, Pittsburgh.
(l-r) L.E. Mc Cullough, D.C. Fitzgerald, Bob Beach, Ernie Hawkins.

Barking Up the Wrong Tree (Reel)

Crisis in Female Sex Hormones (Reel)

The Last Straw (Reel)

The Sporting Lass of Tel Aviv (Reel)

His Own Kind (Reel)

The Sandcutter (Reel)

His Own Kind, front cover outtake, 1981. Photo: Peggi Aloyi.

The Immaculate Deception (Reel)

Devilish Merry, 1979. (l-r) Burr Beard, Jan Hamilton,
L.E. Mc Cullough, Sue Powers, Larry Edelman.
Photo: J. Rafferty

The Wreck of the Nova (Reel)

The Pinsota Fusion (Reel)

Hoosiers in Heat (Reel)

The Humours of Allegheny (Reel)

The Ghost of His Former Self (Reel)

At Odds with Machinery (Reel)

Grits and Kool-Aid (Reel)

Fiddlin' John McGreevy (Reel)

A session at Hoban's Tavern, West 63rd Street, Chicago, 1974.
(l-r) Seamus Cooley, John McGreevy, Paddy Cloonan,
Jimmy Thornton. Photo courtesy Mary Cooley.

30

My Guardian Angel is a Space Cadet (Reel)

Quinlin's Return to Castle Shannon (Reel)

Michael Quinlin (flute) and Seamus Connolly
(fiddle), Prince Edward Island, 1990.
Photo courtesy Michael Quinlin.

The Maiden of Maybury (Reel)

Langley Hall Explosion (Reel)

Late Bloomer (Reel)

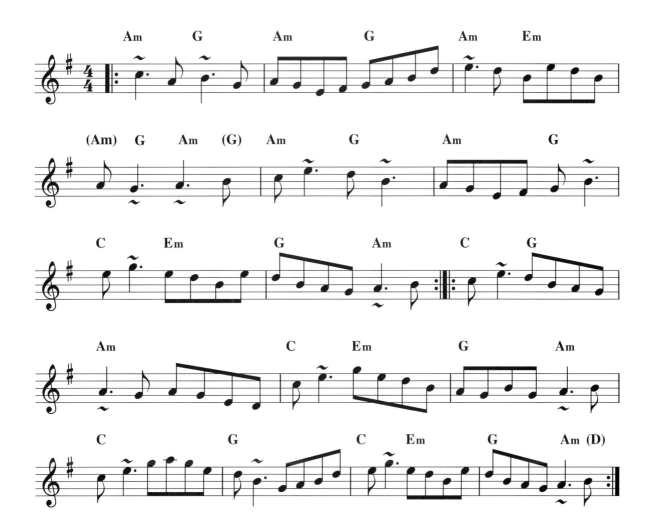

Late Bloomer, 1983. Photo: Jimmy Jalapeño.

Not Safe with a Razor (Reel)

McCullough's Farewell to Pittsburgh (Reel)

Ground Zero (Reel)

The Humours of Sarajevo (Reel)

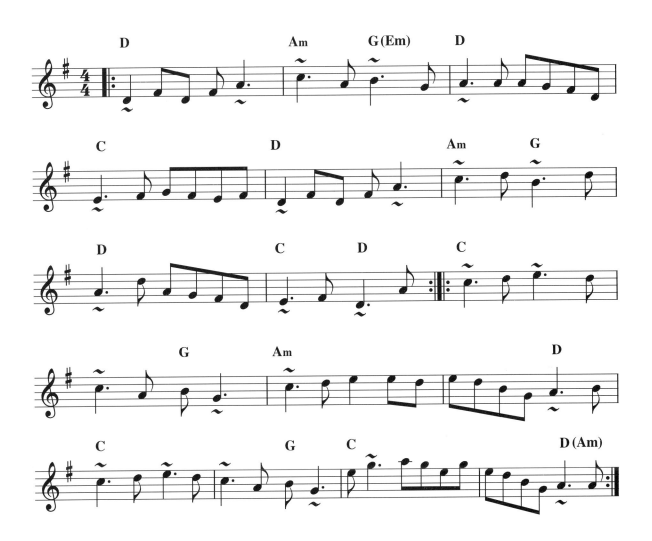

As Good as Gone (Reel)

La Bijoutier (Reel)
(The Gem-Maker)

Cuz from Castleisland (Reel)

Terry Teahan with "Blackie", July, 1976,
Chicago. Photo: L.E. McCullough.

Hammocks go Anywhere (Reel)

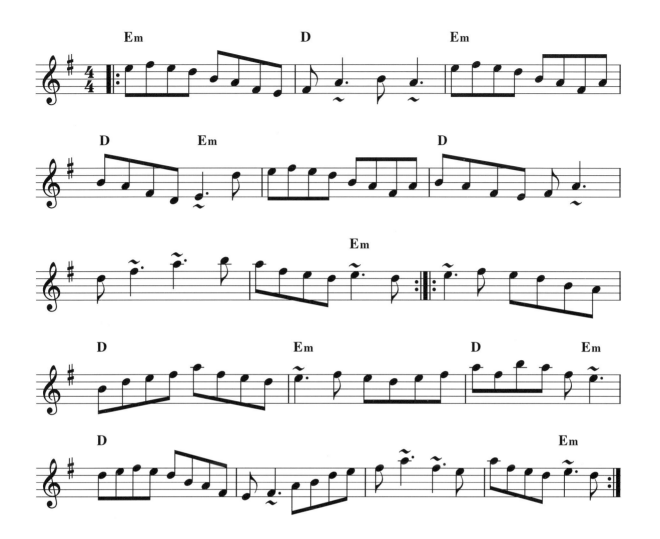

Last Tango in Tarrytown (Reel)

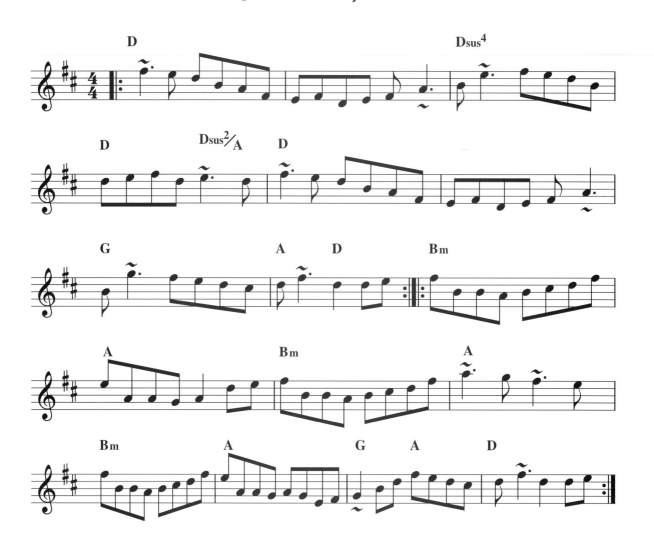

Divin' Ducks, Austin, 1986. (l-r) L.E. McCullough, Marc Schwartz.
Photo: Phil Curry. '57 Cadillac convertible: Sharon Curry.

The Trip to Mesilla (Reel)

Jack and Betty's Boy Bob's Wedding (Hornpipe)

All 65 Pounds of It (March)

Demasiado Corazón (Air)
(Too Much Heart)

Rose Hawkins at age 18. Photo: Joe Hawkins

Birds Sleep Safer on Bellerock Street Tonight
(Hornpipe)

Planxty Linda Fitzpatrick (Planxty)

The Big Bouncy Bag o' Bunny Luv (Polka)

Bunny Luv.
Photo: L.E. McCullough

Famous Last Words (Double Jigs)

The Catnip Lady from Lubbock (Double Jig)

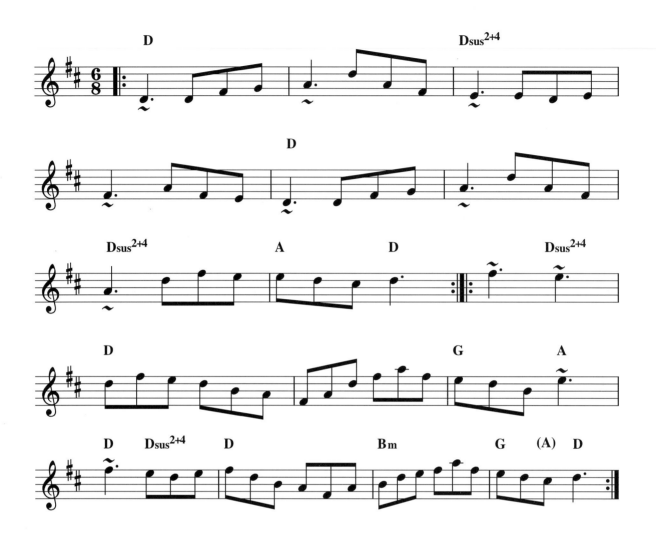

Men and Their Milk Fantasies (Double Jig)

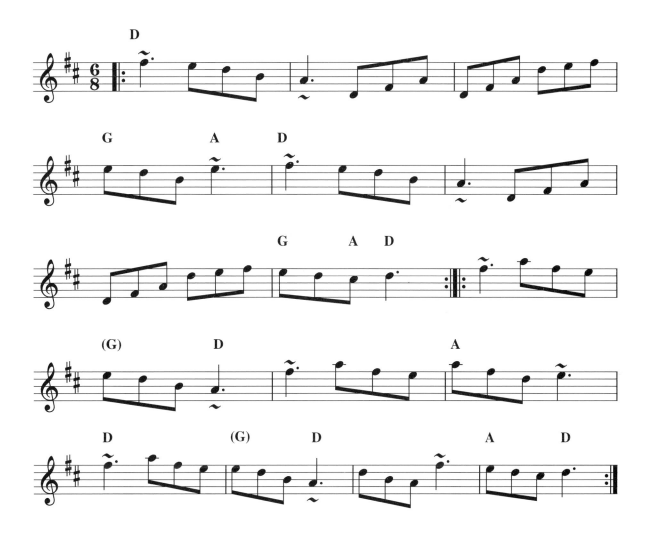

The Middletown Meltdown (Double Jig)

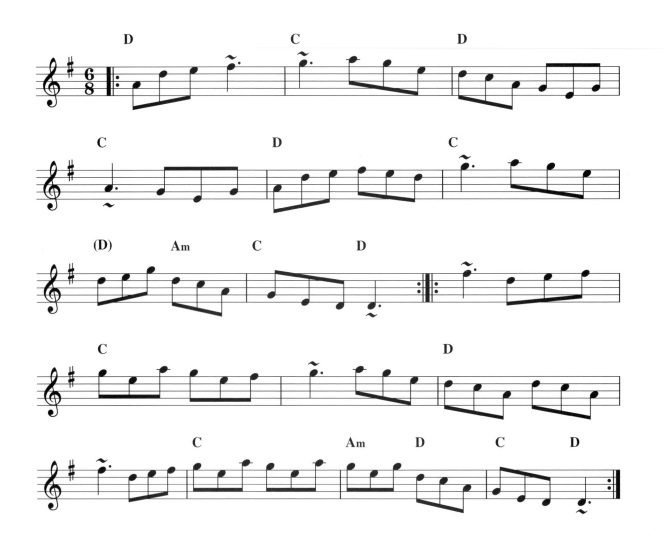

Gassed and Gone (Double Jig)

Gassed and Gone.
Photo: L.E. McCullough

La Encantadora (Double Jig)
(The Enchantress)

Hanging Out to Dry (Double Jig)

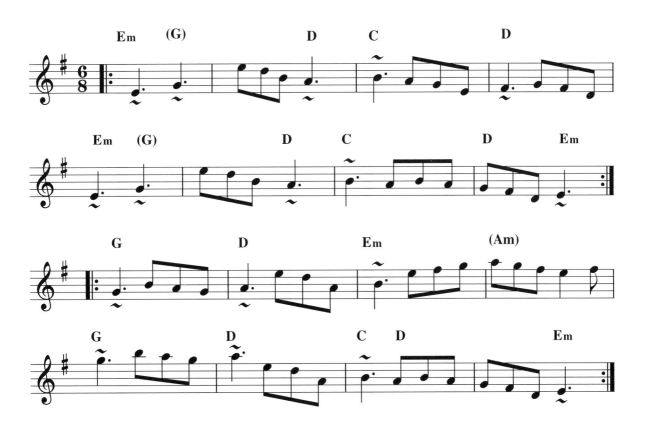

Social Leprosy is on the Rise (Double Jig)

Up to Your Neck in Newts (Double Jig)

L.E. McCullough performing at the White House,
Washington, D.C., 1997.   Photo: Pam Baucom.

Living with the Pack (Set Dance)

Living with the Pack. Photo: L.E. McCullough

Lone Star Rising (Waltz)

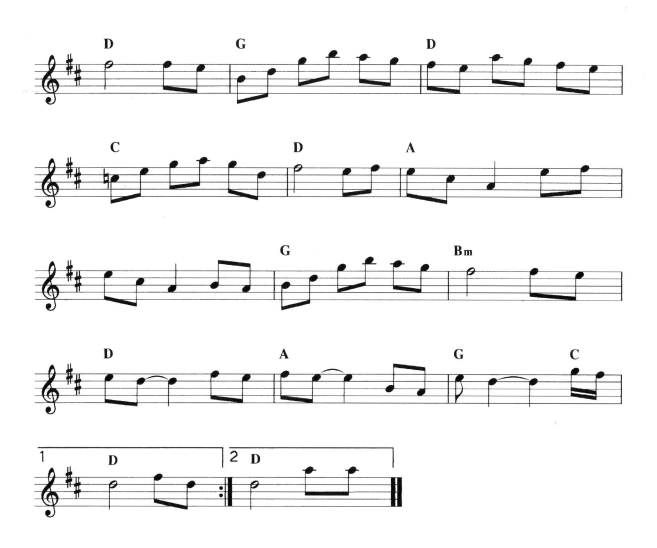

Hally Wood's Fancy (Double Jig)

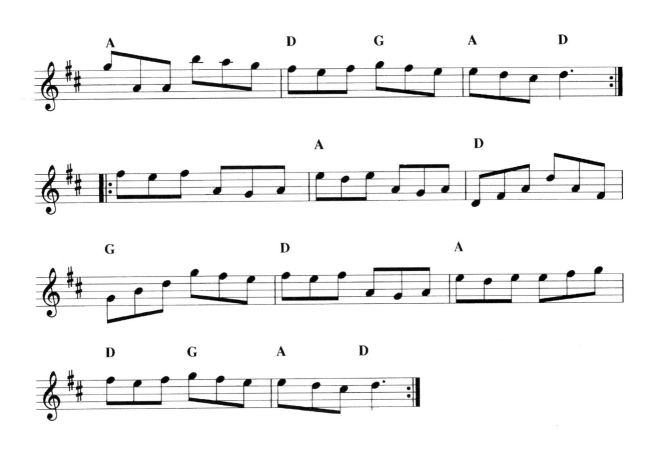

The Sure Way Back (Air)

The Belles of Shadyside (Slip Jig)

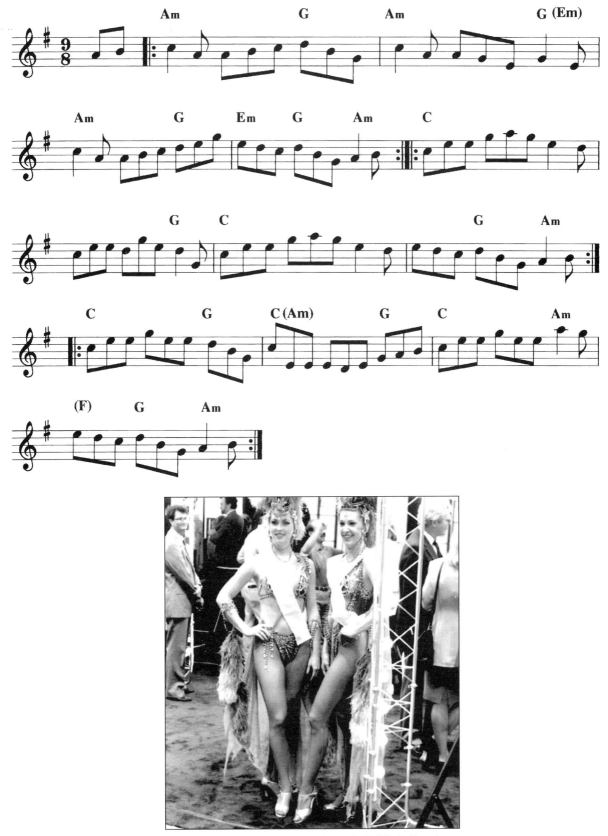

The Belles of Shadyside. Photo: L.E. McCullough

La Polverita Fiera (Waltz)

(The Savage Little Powderpuff)

Looking for the Fifth Foot of the Cat (Courante)

Bourrée Texane, Austin, 1985. (l-r) L.E. McCullough, Lisa Whatley, Sege Lainé

73

Goat Gods and Bean Dip (Waltz)

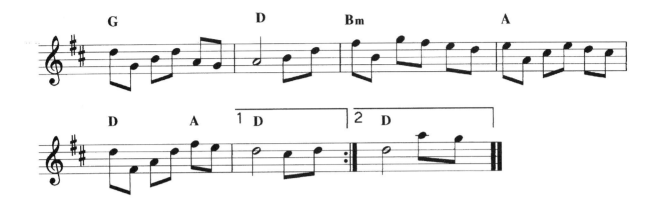

L.E. McCullough. Photo: Brenda K. Michalek.

St. Patrick Was a Cajun (Waltz)

* Repeat A Section
  both times

Paddy Bless the Gumbo (Reel)

Tune Notes

1) The Sporting Lass of Perth/A Snake Is a Chiropractor's Dream/How Much DoThose Weigh?

The Sporting Lass of Perth is dedicated to Janine Burt, a native of Perth, Australia, whom I met hitchhiking on the way to the Fleadh Cheóil na hEireann in 1975. She bought a tinwhistle on the way back to Dublin and, after we returned to our respective hemispheres, wrote me a letter asking for a few tips on learning to play. I provided some and made copies of the correspondence; these transcontinental air-mail lessons evolved into the beginning chapters of *The Complete Irish Tinwhistle Tutor* published a year later. (If any readers have learned to play the whistle from that book, you have an Aussie to thank!) The title of *A Snake Is a Chiropractor's Dream* matches the slithery melodic line and derives from a comment made by chiropractor/guitarist Jeffrey Cohen of Pittsburgh, who has kept numerous Pittsburgh Steelers on the spinal straight and narrow over the years. *How Much Do Those Weigh?* Not a very original introductory line, but surprisingly effective depending upon the lateness of the evening, the fullness of the moon and the quantity of drink taken.

2) Leroy the Barbarian/Corbin's Wedding/Sorry to Meet, Happy to Part

Leroy the Barbarian: imagine a kilt-clad Arnold Schwarzenegger dancing a reel as he whacks off yuppie heads in a suburban Chicago fern bar, and you have an approximate idea of the mayhem that reigned after Pittsburgh blues/ragtime guitarist Ernie Hawkins and I ended a ten-day tour of thirty senior citizen nursing homes and went looking to blow off a little steam. (Who says cinema doesn't incite violence?) *Corbin's Wedding* fluctuates between major and minor modes and was composed the night after I attended the wedding of singer/songwriter Gene Corbin and wife, Vicki, who last I heard were living in Albuquerque, New Mexico. *Sorry to Meet, Happy to Part* is the first traditional Irish tune I ever composed; it likewise alternates between major and minor, much like the romantic relationship that inspired the tune.

3) Barking up the Wrong Tree/Crisis in Female Sex Hormones/The Last Straw

Barking up the Wrong Tree is the third Irish tune I composed and perhaps the most unrelentingly intense; it was written while living in a small town and spending way too much time at Edna's Bare and Ball, a roadside entertainment establishment rarely mentioned in mainstream tour books. *Crisis in Female Sex Hormones* is a reel that tends to be played somewhat slowly before building up steam and catching fire; it was composed during the Ice Age winter of 1978. *The Last Straw* is dedicated to a former housemate named Debbie (can't recall her last name, sorry) who was so thrilled about breaking up with her boyfriend she nearly floated out of the room.

4) The Sporting Lass of Tel Aviv/His Own Kind/The Sandcutter

The first two tunes were composed about an hour after I awoke on the morning following a very long St. Patrick's Day night, inspired by the two ladies with whom I found myself sharing an apartment house stair — Daphna Czernobilsky, an actress and director now teaching in Berlin, Germany, and Adrienne Johnson, last witnessed in Ithaca, New York. *His Own Kind* seems to be an attempt to make a workable dance tune with as few as total notes as possible, in this case, seven. *The Sandcutter* is dedicated to pianist Jan Goering of Austin, Texas; the title refers to a 19th-century cowboy expression for a native of Kansas.

5) The Immaculate Deception/The Wreck of the Nova/The Pinsota Fusion

The Immaculate Deception was composed on Friday the 13th with a black cat sitting on my lap and a big pot of trouble muffin stew simmering on the oven. *The Wreck of the Nova* is an example of the compositional process operating during extreme trauma. On a misty grey morning in the industrial outlands of suburban ChiWorld, my '73 Blue Thunder Chevy Nova entered hyperspace at ramming speed and collided with an alien starfleet Olds 98 — a basic fender-bender that left me outwardly dazed and confused but inwardly strangely attuned to a whole new level of deep sound and melodic stimulation. I'd been on my way to Terry "Cuz" Teahan's house (see *Cuz from Castleisland*), so I whipped out my whistle and composed this tune, drawing curious stares from bystanders and the EMS crew. People tell me this tune casts a weird, otherwordly spell; they never even saw the repair bill. *The Pinsota Fusion* celebrates the wedding of Ernie Sota and Jan Hamilton, who served as sound man and fiddler, respectively, of the group Devilish Merry.

6) Hoosiers in Heat/The Humours of Allegheny/The Ghost of His Former Self

A companion piece to mandolinist Larry Edelman's reel *Hoosiers at Home* (see his *Timepieces* album on D&R Records), *Hoosiers in Heat* was composed after observing the exuberant mating rituals of the clientele at a retro-disco nightclub in downtown Indianapolis. *The Humours of Allegheny* and *The Ghost of His Former Self* were composed on nights when you're too tired to sleep, and the music just slides out of the whistle like you're in somebody else's dream anyway.

7) At Odds with Machinery/Grits and Kool-Aid/Fiddlin' John McGreevy

At Odds with Machinery was composed after having just returned from the pleasant green fields of Ireland to the belching steel town of Pittsburgh following the 1975 Fleadh Ceoil; it's one of those tunes expressing that feeling of being caught in the middle, torn between two possible paths, being held down but almost breaking free, a destiny-vision kind of thing that seems really important at the time but resolves itself in a totally trivial manner a day or two later. *Grits and Kool-Aid*. . . not just for breakfast anymore — a surefire substitute for the hair of the dog when your stomach feels like it's digesting broken glass. *Fiddlin' John McGreevy* is a tribute to one of the most congenial and talented musicians who ever walked the planet. McGreevy was a stalwart maintainer of Irish traditional music in Chicago from the 1930s till his death in 1990 at age 71. His patience with beginning musicians and all-around good humor were legendary (for another McGreevy-inspired tune, see fiddler Liz Carroll's *That's Right, Too* on the first Trian album with Billy McComiskey and Dáithí Sproule).

8) My Guardian Angel Is a Space Cadet/Quinlin's Return to Castle Shannon/The Maiden of Maybury

The "angel" phenomenon has swept through American popular culture with a heavenly vengeance during the 1990s. If one accepts the idea, hypothetically-speaking, that humans do have some spirit guardian, every now and again you have to wonder how well equipped and efficient they are. *Quinlin's Return to Castle Shannon* was composed for the occasion of a welcome home party for Michael Quinlin, a Pittsburgh-born flute player and *Irish Echo* journalist now living in Boston. *The Maiden of Maybury* is the fourth-ever Irish tune I composed back when I still believed that A dorian reels were the most incredible achievement of the human musical mind; dedicated to M. Boynton Wallace.

9) The Langley Hall Explosion/Late Bloomer/Not Safe with a Razor

Shortly after noon on a bitterly cold January day as I was finishing the last edits on the cassette tape to *The Complete Irish Tinwhistle Tutor*, I heard a dull *boom*! and felt the room shake. Earthquakes in the Alleghenies? Not likely. A mile away on the University of Pittsburgh campus, a lecture hall crowded with students had disintegrated into charred rubble; a gas line break caused the explosion that killed two people and injured sixty-eight. That night, pondering upon the absolute immutability of chance, this tune came out. *Late Bloomer* is that feeling you sometimes have that life's train has pulled out of the station, and you're locked in the bathroom with your pants down and no paper on the roll. I can't name real names here, but *Not Safe with a Razor* derives from a night at an especially gruesome honky tonk outside Houston, Texas, when one of our band members we'll call 'Jean-Pierre' exhibited an extreme infatuation toward a female patron possessing six-inch black stiletto nails, breath that could scorch paint at ten feet and enough tattoos to cover a circus tent. "What do you think?" he whispered to Tiny, the six-foot-eight-inch, 300-pound, glass-eyed bouncer, as we packed up for the evening. "Should I go for it?" "Well, son," said Tiny, calmly caressing the sawed-off pool cue in his belt, "there's two kinds of women down here in Texas. One kind is the girl you'd take home to see your momma. . . sweet, gentle, trust her with your last penny and know she'll be there for you come hell or high water." "And the other kind?" Jean-Pierre asked. "The other kind," replied Tiny, "is what you call 'not safe with a razor'. And, son, you look like you bleed awful easy."

10) McCullough's Farewell to Pittsburgh/Ground Zero/The Humours of Sarajevo

McCullough's Farewell to Pittsburgh can be played either slowly or not; it was composed as I prepared to move to Chicago to document the life and craftsmanship of uilleann pipemaker Patrick Hennelly for a National Endowment for the Arts project. *Ground Zero*, composed on the 32nd anniversary of the atomic bombing of Hiroshima, hovers between the I and the VII scale points throughout — tonal ground zero (maybe it's a 24-bar meltdown of Penderecki's *Threnody*). *The Humours of Sarajevo* is a tune that pops out when you realize it's going to take a lot of music by a lot of players all over the world to set people in Bosnia, Belfast, Beirut, Burundi, Burma, etc. marching to the same drummer.

11) As Good As Gone/La Bijoutier/Cuz from Castleisland

As Good As Gone begins as a fairly normal G major, mostly pentatonic reel but strikes off on a more adventurous, somewhat fiddlistic path in the B part; it was composed on the day I decided to return to my hometown after a 20-year absence. I've always liked the boisterous, Celtic-rooted energy of French Canadian music, and *La Bijoutier* is dedicated to Robin Arnold, a jewelry-maker and daughter of a one-time Miss Midland, Texas, who took me to my very first Psychic Fair. (But you already knew that, didn't you?). *Cuz from Castleisland* was named for Chicago concertina/accordion player Terry Teahan (1905-1989), a Kerry native and pupil of Patrick O'Keefe who was an inspiration to many young players throughout the years. Cuz composed a tune for me in his own book, *The Road to Glountane*; I returned the favor shortly after.

12) Hammocks Go Anywhere/Last Tango in Tarrytown/The Trip to Mesilla

Hammocks Go Anywhere is another moody tundra tune from the glacial winter of 1978, the type of edgy, cabin-fever music that emerges when you've been entombed by snow and ice for way too long. By contrast, *Last Tango in Tarrytown* was composed on one of the loveliest autumn mornings I've ever experienced after one of the weirdest autumn evenings I've ever experienced. *The Trip to Mesilla* recalls a concert trip with the French traditional music band Bourrée Texane into the beautiful desert countryside of southern New Mexico at the behest of Marc and Tina Schwartz, organizers of the annual Mesilla Valley Bluesfest.

13) Jack and Betty's Boy Bob's Wedding/All 65 Pounds of It

Jack and Betty's Boy Bob's Wedding is a nuptial gift for some loyal folks who showed up at The Irish Airs' weekly gig at Dooley O'Toole's every single Wednesday for three years. *All 65 Pounds of It* is a march,with some admitted ragtime influence; the title refers to the average portage weight of a Lyon-Healy pedal harp (*sans* cover).

14) Demasiado Corazón/Birds Sleep Safer on Bellerock Street Tonight

Demasiado Corazón should be played with lots of rubato and fermata, slides and slurs, sweetness and soul. I composed it one night for no particular reason and then forgot about it for eight years. About five minutes after I met my wife, Jane, for the first time, it popped back into my head, and I realized I'd been saving it for her. *Birds Sleep Safer on Bellerock Street Tonight* is a tribute to one of the most special cats I've ever known, Rose Hawkins. Up until the very hour of her passing of natural causes at age 20, she was still terrorizing (and often devouring) any animal who dared enter her yard. The tune began as an air, then slipped into a hornpipe, a conscious effort to evoke a cat stalking its prey.

15) Planxty Linda Fitzpatrick/The Big Bouncing Bag o' Bunny Luv

An Anglicization of the Irish word "sláinte", a common salutation meaning "to your health", *planxty* is a tune type that flourished in Ireland during the late 17th and early 18th centuries, particularly among harpers such as Turlough Carolan who composed special pieces in honor of their patrons. *Planxty Linda Fitzpatrick* is a commissioned piece I wrote for a patron of the folk arts in Pittsburgh who was also an outstanding fretted dulcimer player. I tried to keep the melody light and spirited to match the buoyant personality of the lady herself, while sticking as close as possible to the formal, quasi-Baroque structure of the traditional planxty form. I chose key of D major so it would be easily playable on the dulcimer; a few harp-like touches are sprinkled throughout in deference to the genre's origins. *The Big Bouncing Bag o' Bunny Luv* was written for a longtime friend, Jeff Chiplis of Cleveland, who besides being a well-known sculptor and neon artist is also the world's foremost collector of carrot bags.

16) Famous Last Words/The Catnip Lady from Lubbock

Famous Last Words was the first double jig I ever composed; it would be four years and twenty-seven tunes (all reels) before I'd compose another: *The Catnip Lady from Lubbock*, inspired by a fine artist and illustrator, Nancy Joy Perkins. A couple days after meeting her at a Halloween square dance, I received a mysterious package on my doorstep containing a child's sock with about a pound of fresh-pulled catnip sewn inside — a gift for the household's feline contingent, and the trademark calling card of a very unique woman.

17) Men and Their Milk Fantasies/The Middletown Meltdown

Men and Their Milk Fantasies is a bonafide dream tune, a compositional method often found in other cultures but not so frequently in ours. Following a performance at a seaside bar called Anna Christie's, our band flopped down in a fleabag motel on the outskirts of New London, Connecticut, and I dreamed I was playing in a session at which this tune was being played over and over and over. I awoke, went out to the parking lot and it was in my fingers and out the whistle, exactly as I'd heard it in my dream. *The Middletown Meltdown* was inspired by the Three Mile Island nuclear accident outside Harrisburg, Pennsylvania; the fact that the government might lie about such a thing panicked and outraged a lot of people at the time. These days we seem content to live with a lot more "official" lies and enough radiation from personal computers to start your own power plant-in-a-pocket.

18) Gassed and Gone/La Encantadora/Hanging Out to Dry

Gassed and Gone was composed after I'd just arrived in the Catskill Mountains to manage an artist colony. Early in the misty morning, I stood on the front porch and watched a cloud stroll through the front lawn, thinking of my father's ancestors who had passed through this very area in the late 1600s. *La Encantadora* is a double jig with close connections to the Mexican huapango, a dance tune genre also in 6/8; it was inspired after a trip to Corpus Christi as the guest of a young lady from Piedras Negras, Mexico. *Hanging Out to Dry* is an intense, insistent, ticked-off tune about nothing in particular and everything in general.

19) Social Leprosy Is on the Rise/Up to Your Neck in Newts

Social Leprosy Is on the Rise is a tune that just didn't want to quit; if I hadn't been called to the phone, it might have rambled on forever. *Up to Your Neck in Newts* derives its title from the Bing Crosby/Ingrid Bergman film *The Bells of St. Mary's* — "You'll soon be up to your neck in nuns", the rectory housekeeper warns the new priest, Fr. O'Malley. After three years of Newts in Congress, I'll take nuns any day.

20) Living with the Pack

Living with the Pack reflects a lot of teenage listening to the early Dave Brubeck Quartet; think of alto sax wizard Paul Desmond with a whistle. The tune is cast in set dance form, which means the B part has an irregular number of bars — thirty-three in this case, which may be what anthropologists call a 'cultural implant', stemming from the fact I was born in Speedway and there are thirty-three cars in the opening Indy 500 field. Anybody want to create a set dance for it? Be my guest.

21) Lone Star Rising/Hally Wood's Fancy

These tunes were commissioned by folk singer Tanne Ryland of Austin, Texas, to commemorate her mother and father, John Henry Faulk and Hally Wood. *Lone Star Rising* commemorates Faulk, a Texas actor, writer and humorist who became a nationally-known First Amendment spokesman after fighting and surviving the notorious McCarthy Era blacklist. Wood was a banjoist/folklorist who, during her New York City days with John Henry, hung out and played with Woody Guthrie, Leadbelly, Cisco Houston, the Weavers and other American folk music icons of the 1940s. I had the pleasure of meeting her once at a session at the Colorado Street Cafe in Austin, and this tune is something she would have enjoyed plucking out on the banjo; there's a bit of Mexican influence, too, to make her feel at home in her native South Texas.

22) The Sure Way Back/The Belles of Shadyside

The Sure Way Back is an air derived from the double jig *Gassed and Gone*. I created it for *Alien to New York*, a film by Big Apple filmmaker Anna Holland about a young Irishman who emigrates to New York, gets AIDS and dies. It ain't no bucket of grins, but the music was scored by keyboardist Thomas Newton, and it has some very fine cinematic moments. In the late 1970s the Shadyside Arts Festival was a huge weekend-long block party that featured arts, crafts, entertainment and the heady allure of instant summer romance. *The Belles of Shadyside* was originally written as a reel, then eased into a slip jig structure.

23) La Polverita Fiera/Looking for the Fifth Foot of the Cat

La Polverita Fiera was named for an amazing pastel calico kitten who once owned me; as an actual dance tune, it's been used primarily by ballet dancers. *Looking for the Fifth Foot of the Cat* began life as a letter-head. I received a note from harpist Julia Sanders of Houston written on stationary that had a little music staff with treble clef notes sprinkled on it in no meter or obvious key; I worked the notes (B, C, D, E) into a melody in B minor with a courante rhythm probably influenced by the French traditional music group with whom I was performing at the time. The title is a colloquial expression in Spanish ("buscando la quinta pata al gato") akin to the English "going on a wild goose chase", according to Austin singer/guitarist Pipo Hernandez, a native of the Canary Islands.

24) Goat Gods and Bean Dip/St. Patrick Was a Cajun/Paddy Bless the Gumbo

Goat Gods and Bean Dip is a waltz with a slight stagger here and there, written after I went bowling for the first time as an adult above the age of supposed reason. *St. Patrick Was a Cajun* derives from the line Colm Meany utters in the film *The Commitments* to a young bloke asserting that Meany's messiah, Elvis Presley, was from Louisiana. "Blasphemy!" snarls the offended and xenophobic Meany. "Elvis was no f***in' Cajun!". Too bad for Elvis, because Cajun music and Cajun culture are among the most magnificent in the world; this tune is dedicated to all musicians who have extended their music beyond the limits of their inherited tradition. The air can be played as a straight Irish waltz or with some serious seasoning *á la bayou*, then shifted into a Cajun two-step or an Irish reel — *Paddy Bless the Gumbo* — depending upon whether you want to be in Louisiana or Ireland at the moment.

Some Observations
on L.E. McCullough's Composing Process:
An Interview with Dena Chandler

DC: Discussions of an individual's compositional style typically begin with an examination of the composer — his family upbringing, musical training, unique life experiences and so forth. What can you tell us about you?

LEM: Not much, really. I am a middle-aged American born in the middle of the 20th century to a middle-class family living in the middle of Middle America. I've always been an extremely ordinary person and had very ordinary experiences growing up; my parents put a piano in the living room when I was eight, so I took lessons, started giving recitals and just pretty much always thought about music a lot from then on. Mostly classical, jazz, rock and blues on piano, saxophone, clarinet, recorder, guitar and harmonica.

DC: Was traditional Irish music in your family at all?

LEM: I am third-generation Irish on my mother's side; the Igoes, Tracys, Doyles, McDermotts and Healys arrived in Brooklyn during the 1890s, but they assimiliated fairly quickly. My grandfather Igoe was a big Caruso fan, and my Uncle Larry loved Elvis. I never heard anything remotely resembling traditional Irish music or song until I went to Ireland at age nineteen.

DC: Do you remember the first time you heard it?

LEM: The first music I heard on Radio Éireann on the way in from the airport was *Breathless* by Jerry Lee Lewis; traditional music wasn't very present in the mainstream Irish media back then. I didn't hear any Irish music for over a month, until one night when I stumbled — literally — into a session at O'Donoghue's Pub. Jammed into the corner by the front window, completely surrounded by a cheering crowd, were John Kelly, Sr. and Joe Ryan on fiddles, Peter Phelan on uilleann pipes, Paddy O'Brien the Younger on accordion, Mary Bergin on tinwhistle, Mick O'Connor on flute and Owen Pender on guitar. I'd walked into one of the hottest sessions in town, and I'll never forget the way that music thrilled me. Curiously, it was October 3, 1971, the same day the great Irish composer and traditional music revivalist Seán Ó Riada died in London.

DC: How did you relate to this new musical phenomenon?

LEM: I'd heard echoes of it in bluegrass and Appalachian music, but jigs and reels and slow airs in their more or less pristine state just blew my mind. My parents got me a small cassette recorder for Christmas, and I hitchhiked around Ireland for months taping every traditional singer and musician I could find. I had the incredible good fortune to meet scholars like Breandán Breathnach, Hugh Shields, Tom Munnelly, Seán O'Sullivan, Brian Boydell, Terry Moylan and John Kelly and his family. Paddy Moloney spent an hour talking to me one day in the Claddagh Records office on Dame Street. They were all an incredible fount of knowledge. I'm sure they were quite amused that some kid from Indiana was knocking about in search of the Irish music grail, but I was obsessed.

DC: When did you start actually playing Irish music?

LEM: When I came back to the States in July, 1972. Because I already played wind instruments, I took up the tinwhistle as my entrée into Irish music. I spent the next two years simply trying to reproduce the tunes and the playing styles I heard. I copied tunes off records and from musicians I taped at sessions note-for-note, which was quite a change. Before, I'd been entranced by the improvisatory freedom of jazz and progressive rock; now it was the stringent discipline of Irish music that intrigued me — how infinitely more challenging it was to express your musical individuality within the limited metric and melodic confines of a 16-bar jig, reel or hornpipe.

DC: When did you decide to compose tunes in the Irish idiom?

LEM: I'm not sure I consciously decided, Dena. I mean, the notion to compose new music in this centuries-old tradition didn't occur to me until I'd learned a few hundred "standards". Then, one day I was fooling around with the whistle, maybe playing *The Sligo Maid* or something, the first few notes of a new tune came out and sounded good. . . sounded somehow different from the other tunes I knew. . . and I decided to try and make a whole tune just to finish what I'd started. Within an hour I had scratched down the notes of a two-part reel on some music notation paper; a couple days later I had it memorized and took to playing it for friends around town. They liked it, and I realized I could compose a new tune that worked. It was another way to be involved with the music.

DC: That was 1974. Since then you've composed 78 tunes in traditional Irish formats.

LEM: Probably a couple more I forgot to write down or tape, so they're lost forever. But 78 is how many I've figured were worth keeping.

DC: Were there peak years for new tunes?

LEM: The 1970s were big. I composed ten each in '77 and '78, something like 43 from '74 to '79. I pretty much lived and breathed Irish music then. In 1980 I started playing more blues and ragtime, and then I moved to Texas in '83, where I started getting into French, Cajun, Mexican, African music and so on. From then on I composed usually for a specific purpose, a commission, say, whereas in the '70s the tunes just poured out of me for no real reason at all.

DC: What made you sit down and compose a tune?

LEM: The first one, as I said, just happened. After that I found myself using tunes to convey personal feelings and moods. Or to commemorate events in my life or the larger world. If it was somebody's birthday or wedding, and you didn't have money for a present, you could give them a tune, like the old harpers who composed tunes for patrons. I've written tunes about people dying, people getting born. A car wreck I had. Natural disasters. Parties. Road trips with the band. A moronic club owner I played for once. And cats. I wrote several tunes about cats.

DC: A number of your tunes, judging by the titles, seem to refer to romantic relationships of one sort or another.

LEM: Yeh, well, in ancient Ireland they apparently had three types of music: *goltraí*, which was for making people sad, *geantraí* which made people laugh and *suantraí*, which supposedly induced sleep. I guess I added a fourth category — *suirgtraí*, the attempt to induce love.

DC: Can you describe the actual process of how you compose a tune?

LEM: The process begins with motivation. Some tunes you consciously compose for some reason or another, because you've been commissioned or because you want to mark some occasion or whatever. Others just emerge from your instrument when you're relaxing and have no specific purpose to satisfy. With the "accidental" tunes, what happens is a riff pops out, maybe two bars. Take the reel *Last Tango in Tarrytown* as an example. I picked up the flute one day and was just doing rolls up and down the scale, when I played the first two bars.

Bars 1and 2 of *Last Tango in Tarrytown*

I mean, they just were there. The riff begins with a long roll and ends with a long roll; bars 1 and 2 are like mirror images of each other. That sounded interesting, so I repeated it a couple times, and I got the urge to keep going. I spun out another two bars that sort of answered the first two, and I had a phrase with some basic melodic direction.

Bars 3 and 4 of *Last Tango in Tarrytown*

The first phrase had ended on the second tone of the scale, so it was asking to be resolved to the tonic. There are several ways to do this in a reel, but the way I chose here was to start the second phrase by bringing the harmonic path back to tonic, or D major, by repeating the first two bars.

Bars 5 and 6 of *Last Tango in Tarrytown*

Then, the concluding two bars of the second phrase would be a variant of the melodic material in bars 3 and 4. Instead of going from the B to the E long roll, I went to the G which led the melody in the same rising direction as before but went higher — surprise! a little extra tension and uncertainty here — before descending back down to the tonic.

Bars 7 and 8 of *Last Tango in Tarrytown*

DC: So you had the first part then.

LEM: Right. And to lead off the second part I went to a B minor triad, which is the relative minor key to D major. Moving between relative major and minor or minor to major when you change A and B parts is a move that happens a fair amount in Irish dance tunes. I use it in 27 of the 78 tunes. It seems to ratchet up the excitement real quick and then, of course, you resolve back to the tonic at the end of the B part.

Bars 9 -12 of *Last Tango in Tarrytown*

The melody in the first bar of the B part was over a B minor triad, so the second bar went to an A major chord with the melody resolving on A; I kept this basic B minor to A major harmonic movement through the next four bars before going back to the G-A-D harmonic pattern in bars 15 and 16, matching the way the A part had ended. But the actual melody in bars 11 and 12 is different from bars 9 and 10, even though they have the same harmonic base. Bar 11 repeats bar 9, but bar 12 hits the high A note and holds the F# to end the phrase. Bars 13 and 14 are basically a repeat of bars 9 and 10, except that bar 14 doesn't pause on the quarter note A; the melody is all eighths and keeps moving rhythmically forward, sliding into the G of bar 15 that kicks into the concluding phrase of the B part.

Bars 13-16 of *Last Tango in Tarrytown*

DC: How much of this structure is calculated? How much just ends up working out?

LEM: It's all calculated in that I made deliberate choices to put one note after another in a particular order, but, no, as I was spinning the tune out for the first time I did not consciously say, "Okay, let's balance this B minor triad with A major" or, "Hey, let's modulate from major to minor at the B part." The melody comes out as you feel it, and it assumes its direction and shape more or less automatically as you try and make it fit the preconceived format you have of what a reel is or what a jig is. After you've been playing the music a while and you know what its accepted structures are, you tend to fit your new melody into the pattern as you're creating it. By the rules of the idiom you know where you have to end up in each 8-bar section, and you know where you've started, so the job is to fill in the space between the two points with a melody that has a logic to its movement. . . a logic that other players and listeners besides you can understand.

DC: You know where you're going but never quite sure how you'll be getting there.

LEM: Right. And of course, we've explored only one way to play the tune. You can introduce melodic and rhythmic variations in your basic melody and still stay within the same harmonic structure and even maintain most of the melodic markers that define the overall melodic movement and character of the tune. Say you played bars 9 and 10 like this:

or this:

or even this:

It's really the same tune, and the variations haven't changed the tune's overall identity. Obviously, the variation process is too complex to go into here, but Irish music is incredibly flexible in that area.

DC: Is the composing process different with the non-accidental tunes?

LEM: With "planned" tunes, the motivating factor is always different, and you have more initial choices on how to structure the tune. For *Lone Star Rising*, which was written to commemorate John Henry Faulk of Texas, I wanted something that sounded kind of "Texan" — vaguely American country-western yet stately, heroic, like a cowboy loping along the wide-open range. I chose a waltz meter and kept the A part melody simple and straightforward, no big jumps or excessive step-wise runs. And in the concluding phrase, I hit the tonic note three times in four bars with a syncopated eighth-to-dotted quarter figure that slams down hard and conveys Faulk's strength in surviving all the political persecution he endured. At least that's what was in my mind when I composed it. Who knows what anybody else thinks when they hear it. As Debussy said, "Works of art make rules, but rules do not make works of art."

Cuz from Castleisland was written for Terry Teahan. I tried to portray his ebullient personality, so the tune is in a major key all the way through. I don't think I ever heard him play a minor or modal tune; even when he did, I seem to remember they sounded major, anyway. To invoke the sound of his accordion pushing and pulling in and out, I worked the notes of the D triad against the A note in a kind of pedal point. Tunes like *The Middletown Meltdown, Ground Zero, The Humours of Sarajevo* are basically about pretty downer topics, and they end up being in D mixolydian, which seems to cast a reflective sort of mood.

DC: Was that the emotional effect you were looking for?

LEM: I guess. They affect me emotionally, but the subjectivity of all this is pretty staggering. Nobody ever hears the same piece of music the same way as anyone else, so it's really impossible to postulate a grand design for what the melody of a tune "means". I mean, *The Foxhunter's Reel* might conjure up the image of a fox hunt in your mind; but what if you heard it by another title — say, *The Roofthatcher's Reel*? Or *The Pawnbroker's Reel*? Or *The Headhunter's Reel*? The meaning in your mind might change, even though the actual tune was the same. When you analyze Irish dance music, all you really can do is take notice of the patterns that occur in a body of tunes and perhaps compare them to another similar body of tunes. I did an analysis of the tunes in Ed Reavy's tunebook *Where the Shannon Rises* a few years ago and found that 47% of his dance tunes shift to a mixolydian mode at some point in the tune; about 15% of Irish dance tunes in the larger tradition are mixolydian. That's a definite pattern, but we don't know what that particular pattern meant to Reavy or if he was even aware of it.

DC: What are some noticeable patterns in your tunes?

LEM: In terms of modality, about 40% are major, 25% dorian, 18% minor and the rest mixolydian. Almost 22% of the major tunes are in D, 21% in G. All the dorian tunes are in A. There are 19 of them and 17 are reels, all of which were composed from 1974-80 and nary a one since, so you could say I went through an especially intense A dorian reel phase in my dissipated youth.

I tend to compose reels. 53 of the 78 tunes — that's over two-thirds — are reels. The next closest genre is double jigs, and there are 10 of those. I don't know how that compares to other contemporary composers of Irish dance tunes. I guess most of the genuinely "mood" tunes I compose take shape as reels. Formwise, they mostly all conform to the standard two-part AB section structure. I've got a three-part hornpipe, a three-part reel, a four-part double jig, a three-part slip jig and a set dance with a 33-bar B part.

DC: Do you have a wide melodic range or use a lot of melodic pitches per tune?

LEM: The range is limited to what fits comfortably on the tinwhistle or basic flute starting at D above middle C. Two tunes reach as high as second-octave C#, one C natural, the rest are B or below. Fifty-six of the tunes have D above middle C as the bottom note; only one tune doesn't rise to G or higher. Two-thirds of the tunes use between 10 and 12 pitches, only two use 14 pitches, only one 15 and one 7. In terms of the scale pitches, 14 are pentatonic, 29 hexatonic, 34 heptatonic. One tune, *All 65 Pounds of It*, has nine scale notes because it has a C# and an F natural in the key of G major; it's the only tune that uses chromatic notes.

DC: What about the actual melodic material?

LEM: There are 11 scale patterns used. The regular 1-2-3-4-5-6-7 pattern predominates 44% of the time. 1-2-3-4-5-7 and 1-2-3-5-6-7 are the next most common. All the tunes have a tonic and dominant pitch. Only 10 don't have the 1-3-5 tonic triad that appears in most Irish dance music; all of those 10 are reels and 9 are A dorian.

In terms of the melodic material used to construct the A and B sections, the A parts of the tunes make use of seven motive patterns, of which A-B-A-C is the most common (48 of the tunes), A-B-C-D next common (17 tunes) and A-B-A-B after that (13 tunes). The B parts make use of a lot more motive patterns — 41 to be exact, the most common being D-E-D-F and D-E-D-C (12 tunes each) and D-E-F-C (9 tunes). Motives from the A part are also used in the B part of 44 of the 78 tunes, which is a way to tie the B part into A part, especially at the final cadence. I could go on with these statistics forever, but I think you see the drift.

DC: All your tunes have a logical thread tying them together.

LEM: They have several threads and probably several logics. A musicologist named Theodor Reik once wrote that music expresses what people feel rather than what they think. Music doesn't come from conscious thought, but from what he called "the stream of preconsciousness" that's running through our minds all the time.

DC: Are there any other elements you believe determine how you compose a tune?

LEM: Yes. How it feels in the fingers. You can analyze the modes and scales and melodic markers all you want, but I'd say a lot of the tunes just feel good when I play them. I don't know which comes first, Dena: you play the riff because it makes musical sense, or you play it because it feels good in your fingers. But I've never consciously composed something to be difficult or deliberately idiosyncratic. I want these tunes to be played by ordinary musicians. In a couple instances they're being played about and I've already been forgotten as the composer. That's fine, because it means they've joined the active tradition, which for me is the whole point.

DC: How do you write your tunes and preserve them?

LEM: If it's an accidental mood tune, I'll generally get the first part together before I make an effort to write it down. If music paper is handy I put it down on that; if not, I draw staves on any paper available. I've written down first drafts of tunes on paper bags, envelopes, once the inside of a paperback book cover. A couple times I've taped it on a cassette recorder and then transcribed it into notation later. If it's a commission piece or otherwise pre-meditated, I sit down with pen and paper at the start. I use tinwhistle or flute. I've never composed Irish music on any other instrument.

DC: Do you complete the tune all the way through the first time?

LEM: About half the time yes; sometimes I run out of inspiration or get interrupted and come back to it later, a few hours, maybe a few days. I wrote one tune while driving a car and stopped every few blocks to jot it down on a notebook pad. I don't revise much. Only five or six tunes have I radically changed after the first draft. It either works for you at first, and the idea of the melody jells in your mind, or it never will. Once I've settled on a complete version of the tune, I write it out, stick it in a file folder and eventually get around to putting it on the computer.

DC: Have you ever begun with the B part of the tune and worked your way back?

LEM: No. When I'm first hearing the tune, it's the A part.

DC: You stressed your "normality" earlier on, but you've traveled quite widely and performed a variety of musics from different cultures. Surely, some of these influences have shown up in your Irish tunes.

LEM: That's undeniable. But just because I liked the Beach Boys as a kid doesn't mean I think of *Surfin' U.S.A.* when I'm composing a hornpipe. There are only 10 tunes where I purposely incorporated some kind of "foreign" element and only three of those would really stop you cold; the rest are all intended to be played at Irish sessions by Irish musicians. Overall, I'd say an L.E. McCullough tune is pretty close to the norm of other Irish traditional tunes. I don't think the Irish musicians who play them would bother, otherwise.

DC: What sort of reaction do you get when you spring one upon an unsuspecting public?

LEM: If I'm at a session, and I play one of my tunes, somebody will usually say, "I haven't heard that one before. Where did you get it?" — like it's from a record they haven't heard or a tune in O'Neill's they never learned. Or sometimes they say, "That's an old one there. I haven't heard that in years."

DC: You don't mind that they don't know it's your own tune?

LEM: Not at all. That's when I know I've made something worthwhile.

— Dena Chandler is a freelance journalist and choreographer in San Diego, California.

The Tunes: When and Where Composed

A Snake Is a Chiropractor's Dream — 11/29/75, Pittsburgh, Pennsylvania

All 65 Pounds of It — 11/28/83, Austin, Texas

As Good As Gone — 4/27/90, Austin, Texas

At Odds with Machinery — 9/16/76, Pittsburgh, Pennsylvania

Barking Up the Wrong Tree — 6/13/74, Lafayette, Indiana

Belles of Shadyside — 7/29/77, Pittsburgh, Pennsylvania

Big Bouncy Bag o' Bunny Luv — 1/23/95, Woodstock, New York

Birds Sleep Safer on Bellerock Street Tonight — 4/23/88, Austin, Texas

Catnip Lady from Lubbock — 10/27/78, Pittsburgh, Pennsylvania

Corbin's Wedding — 10/25/78, Pittsburgh, Pennsylvania

Crisis in Female Sex Hormones — 1/29/78, Pittsburgh, Pennsylvania

Cuz from Castleisland — 9/19/76, Pittsburgh, Pennsylvania

Demasiado Corazón — 4/5/88, Austin, Texas

Famous Last Words — 9/2/74, Pittsburgh, Pennsylvania

Fiddlin' John McGreevy — 8/16/90, Indianapolis, Indiana

Gassed and Gone — 5/17/94, Palenville, New York

Ghost of His Former Self — 4/7/77, Pittsburgh, Pennsylvania

Goat Gods and Bean Dip — 1/9/88, Austin, Texas

Grits and Kool-Aid — 10/18/78, Pittsburgh, Pennsylvania

Ground Zero — 8/7/77, Pittsburgh, Pennsylvania

Hally Wood's Fancy — 7/15/90, Austin, Texas

Hammocks Go Anywhere — 1/31/78, Pittsburgh, Pennsylvania

Hanging Out to Dry — 5/15/88, Austin, Texas

His Own Kind — 3/20/78, Pittsburgh, Pennsylvania

Hoosiers in Heat — 11/7/90, Indianapolis, Indiana

How Much Do Those Weigh? — 9/7/75, Pittsburgh, Pennsylvania

Humours of Allegheny — 10/3/77, Pittsburgh, Pennsylvania

Humours of Sarajevo — 7/30/93, Indianapolis, Indiana

Immaculate Deception — 4/13/79, Pittsburgh, Pennsylvania

Jack & Betty's Boy Bob's Wedding — 7/30/93, Indianapolis, Indiana

La Bijoutier — 4/24/88, Austin, Texas

La Encantadora — 6/26/88, Austin, Texas

La Polverita Fiera — 12/24/83, Indianapolis, Indiana

Langley Hall Explosion — 1/20/77, Pittsburgh, Pennsylvania

Last Straw — 10/12/81, Pittsburgh, Pennsylvania

Last Tango in Tarrytown — 10/23/87, Austin, Texas

Late Bloomer — 11/16/76, Pittsburgh, Pennsylvania

Leroy the Barbarian — 1/7/79, Pittsburgh, Pennsylvania

Living with the Pack — 6/15/87, Austin, Texas

Lone Star Rising — 7/16/90, Austin, Texas

Looking for the Fifth Foot of the Cat — 11/14/83, Austin, Texas

Maiden of Maybury — 2/9/74, Bloomington, Indiana

McCullough's Farewell to Pittsburgh — 2/19/75, Pittsburgh, Pennsylvania

Men and Their Milk Fantasies — 8/31/79, New London, Connecticut

Middletown Meltdown — 4/5/79, Pittsburgh, Pennsylvania

My Guardian Angel Is a Space Cadet — 2/11/94, Indianapolis, Indiana

Not Safe with a Razor — 10/8/75, Pittsburgh, Pennsylvania

Paddy Bless the Gumbo — 7/18/96, Indianapolis, Indiana

Pinsota Fusion — 8/11/78, Pittsburgh, Pennsylvania

Planxty Linda Fitzpatrick — 5/5/81, Pittsburgh, Pennsylvania

Quinlin's Return to Castle Shannon — 9/3/77, Pittsburgh, Pennsylvania

Sandcutter — 4/11/87, Austin, Texas

Social Leprosy Is on the Rise — 1/14/79, Pittsburgh, Pennsylvania

Sorry to Meet, Happy to Part — 1/23/74, Bloomington, Indiana

Sporting Lass of Perth — 9/5/75, Dublin, Eire

Sporting Lass of Tel Aviv — 3/20/78, Pittsburgh, Pennsylvania

St. Patrick Was a Cajun — 1/22/95, Athens, New York

The Sure Way Back — 12/14/94, Athens, New York

Trip to Mesilla — 3/31/90, Las Cruces, New Mexico

Up to Your Neck in Newts — 8/26/90, Indianapolis, Indiana

Wreck of the Nova — 5/2/76, Chicago, Illinois

Discography: L.E.McCullough

(year / title / performer / label; * denotes solo recording)

	1975	*Hollow Poplar*, anthology (Log Cabin)
	1976	*Ladies on the Flatboat*, anthology (Log Cabin)
*	**1977**	**The Complete Irish Tinwhistle Tutor (Silver Spear)**
	1978	*Smoky City Folk Festival*, anthology (Wildebeest)
	1979	*The Ghost of His Former Self*, Devilish Merry (Wildebeest)
	1981	*Ragtime Signatures*, Ernie Hawkins (Wildebeest)
	1982	*Ed Reavy*, anthology (Rounder
*	**1982**	**His Own Kind (Wildebeest)**
	1983	*The Light through the Leaves*, anthology (Rounder)
*	**1984**	**Late Bloomer (Kicking Mule)**
	1985	*Blackbottom Strut*, Dana Hamilton (Sweet Song)
	1985	*Amis, Buvons*, Bourrée Texane (Savage Dumpling)
	1986	*Texican*, Allen Damron (Quahadi)
	1987	*Wild Goose*, Rick Abrams (Heritage)
	1988	*Timepieces*, Larry Edelman (D&R)
*	**1988**	**Favorite Irish Session Tunes (Homespun)**
	1988	*Store Bought Cookies*, Alison Rogers (Bumbadeeda)
	1989	*Blue Corn*, Erik Hokkanen (Lone Wolf)
	1989	*Live at Stubbs'*, Jerry Sires & The Stallions (Trail's End)
*	**1989**	**Feadanísta (Bluezette)**
	1990	*"It's Too Much!"*, Too Much (JRH)
	1990	*Nuevos Caminos*, Toqui Amaru (Fuego)
	1991	*Noodle Soup*, Primitive Moderns (Pinnacle)
	1992	*Mojo Marc & Tina*, Divin' Ducks (Searchin' the Desert for the Blues)
	1994	*Connlaoi's Tale: The Woman Who Danced on Waves*, T.H. Gillespie (Ethos)
	1994	*The Best of Kicking Mule Records, Vol. 2,* anthology (LaserLight)
*	**1996**	**Learn to Play Irish Tinwhistle (Homespun)**
	1996	*The West*, soundtrack (Sony Classical)
	1996	*Michael Collins*, soundtrack (Warner Bros.)
	1997	*Lovers' Waltz*, Jay Ungar & Molly Mason (Angel/EMI)
	1997	*The Healing Cup: Guinevere Seeks the Grail*, T.H. Gillespie (Ethos)
	1997	*Lewis and Clark*, soundtrack (RCA)
*	**1998**	**St. Patrick Was a Cajun (Ossian)**

Tune Index

Ossian Publications

Publishers and Distributors of Irish & General Music

*Ossian Publications produce a large range of Irish Music for
traditional & classical instruments as well as collections of
tunes, songs, instruction books and items
on the history of Irish Music.*

*For our complete list of Books, Sheetmusic, Cassettes, CD's etc,
send us an (international) postal reply coupon
and your name and address.*

Ossian Publications Ltd.

*P.O.Box 84, Cork, Ireland
E-mail: ossian@iol.ie
Web: www.ossian.ie*

OSSIAN